Poems Without Rhyme or Reason and a Couple of Yarns

Erin —

Great to share the stage with you.

D<!-- signature -->

Poems Without Rhyme or Reason and a Couple of Yarns

Dan Crane

iUniverse, Inc.
New York Lincoln Shanghai

Poems Without Rhyme or Reason and a Couple of Yarns

Copyright © 2006 by Dan Crane

All rights reserved. No part of this book may be used or reproduced by any means, graphic, electronic, or mechanical, including photocopying, recording, taping or by any information storage retrieval system without the written permission of the publisher except in the case of brief quotations embodied in critical articles and reviews.

iUniverse books may be ordered through booksellers or by contacting:

iUniverse
2021 Pine Lake Road, Suite 100
Lincoln, NE 68512
www.iuniverse.com
1-800-Authors (1-800-288-4677)

ISBN-13: 978-0-595-39884-3 (pbk)
ISBN-13: 978-0-595-84283-4 (ebk)
ISBN-10: 0-595-39884-7 (pbk)
ISBN-10: 0-595-84283-6 (ebk)

Printed in the United States of America

Contents

I. SNOWY PLACES 1
   LAST WINTER UP HERE 2
   UNDERWAY 8
   DOWN FROM THE MOUNTAINS 10
   ONE LAST TRIP 19
   LOOKING BACK 21
   HOW YOU GET TO ALASKA 22
   WILD COUNTRY 26
   GETTING AND SPENDING 28
   FOR BIG DAVE 29
   BROKE-DICK RIDGE 34
   FOR REBECCA YATES 37
   PUSHBUTTON CONTROL 40

II. SUSPEND YOUR DISBELIEF 41
   HARDSCRABBLE LIVES 42
   AND HAST THOU SLAIN THE JABBERWOCK? 47

ABOUT THE AUTHOR 59

ACKNOWLEDGEMENTS

Because I am not the best judge of my own work, I have deferred to others in selecting several of these pieces. "Last Winter Up Here" won the grand prize in the Anchorage Daily News Writing Contest in 2003. "Down from the Mountains" won the 2005 poetry prize in the Homer News. "And hast thou slain the Jabberwock" was published in Gray's Sporting Journal in the summer edition of 1981. A few other selections have won honorable mention here and there. A couple of poems are new and full of hope.

I.
SNOWY PLACES

Poems Without Rhyme or Reason and a Couple of Yarns

LAST WINTER UP HERE

I.

Angry wind
Screams in our stovepipe
Like a lunatic's piccolo.
Empty oil drums
Bang the door
Begging shelter.

Lights turn orange
Then silently expire
Like old drunks in alleys.
We gather candles
Force-feed the fire
Stay close.

Our road glazes and hardens,
Glares at us.
We joke
That just glimpsing it
Is enough to make you
Fall down on the spot.

In Asia
Smart bombs
Probe private places
So nobody
Over there
Jokes about anything.

Dan Crane

In Texas
Accounts go dry
Like the plastic bags
You see beside the roads
Impaled on barbwire
Wind-ripped and spent.

We hear of these things
On a cheap little radio
Dug from a closet
Pregnant with fresh batteries
Its voices
Full of self-importance.

                        II.

At breakfast
Our mutt bums
A chunk of smoked sockeye
Glistens at once
With its oil
And our love.

Distant snow banners
On the Kenai range
Scour stoic peaks
Beyond our windows
Beyond our reach
Beyond our knowing.

Trees explode around us
Grasping at each other
Clinging to wires
Bruising the ground:
Blow-downs made
For a hungry stove.

Our bull goose
Stuffed with bravado
Struts and flaps
Across the driveway
Slips on the ice
Like a clown on skates

Skids twenty feet
In a heap
Feathers and down
Hopelessly cross-threading
His once blaring voice
Turned into a squeaky fan belt.

A morning nip with coffee
Welcomes in the holiday,
Then we plow through drifts
And find our way
To frosty trash bins
Dispose of ribbons and bows.

I rescue an old Coleman
To mate with one at home
Before they both die.
Dumpster diving on Christmas…
I'm just fine with it,
It feels religious.

III.

Some weeks later
A woman in a kayak
On wind-tossed waters
Suffers choking salt
Hands the mystery
Of her dying over

To tides and newsprint.
We see waves from here,
Miles off, and never
Catch her helpless effort
Our focus wrong
Our lens screwed down

To our tight winter world.
We mourn a stranger
The best we can,
But poorly; we crack
A book of celluloid sailors
Our family album

Our boats, our friends,
Our cozy little circle.
What luck
To trick these seas
For thirty years
And wash up here!

Out on the spit
In the pit of night
Lonely lights still pulse
As if that stranger's heartbeat
Beneath those wrinkled waters
Echoes in their filaments.

IV.

Peace descends
In middle February.
Senators and tax collectors
Rub their soft hands.
Women here crowd seeds
Into greenhouse windows.

Our old dozer on snow duty
Starts growling for dirt
On this hillside,
A surly bachelor bear
Shaking off the ice
Of yet another winter.

Dan Crane

Out on the edge
Fresh fish are stirring
In the heavy depths
Moving toward us again
With sex and hunger
In their souls.

We sharpen hooks
Buy a pail of copper paint
Drive down to the boat.
A voice starts
Its ancient whisper
In our blood.

We stir
As dead men jerk
When probes touch nerves
As bulbs break frost
When lava
Rumbles way below.

One morning an egg
Shows up in the duck house…
Our cat slips out
For the first time
Since equinox
And leaps at birds.

Poems Without Rhyme or Reason and a Couple of Yarns

UNDERWAY

Come down
To the boat
With me.
We'll sand the rails
Crimp new hooks
Tinker with taglines.

The sun is back.
At dusk
Molten gold gushes
Down the peaks
And cools itself
In cracks of ice.

Tomorrow
We'll catch the tide
And buck westward
Until the wind stiffens.
Yes, my radios work
But no one talks

Much anymore.
My partners have gone
Bankrupt or crazy
Bitten by fish
Swallowed by boats
Just old broken men.

Dan Crane

But we'll go, you and I,
We'll get our first bite
In a place I know
Forty fathoms deep
And plugged with krill…
Tomorrow.

Poems Without Rhyme or Reason and a Couple of Yarns

DOWN FROM THE MOUNTAINS

A neighbor found him dead
At the bottom
Of his basement stairs
A tooth-marked
Chunk of cheese
In his hand

A head full
Of vein occlusions
A railroad watch
In the bib pocket
Of his coveralls
Ticking just for him.

He went down
In full stride
And lay there some hours
Five feet
From where his dog
Had died…

Old Judy, a slobbering
Bulldog that grieved
Herself to death
Just months before
When Grandma
Didn't make it home.

Dan Crane

So you could say
That everything dead-ended
In an ugly heap
And you could leave
His place that day
Convinced that all

The living
And all the loving
We take on
Add up to nothing
But a pinch
Of that old widower

Broken and lonely
Breathing his last
On a concrete floor
With no one around
To offer succor,
Just a dog's bed

To lie beside
And in the end
To die beside…
But I remember stories
Of other times
Of better times

And I need to think
That he could still remember
Even at the last
Despite the pain
Despite the cold
Back to that time

When he came
Down from the mountains
Above Yankee Doodle Lake
Through Corona Pass and Toland
Straight into the North Yard
At Denver

Picked up an ass-pocket
Full of money from the timekeeper
And promptly spent it
On brand new furniture
For his whole house,
Blew his overtime windfall in a day!

Stuck at the summit
For four days and nights
Because the rotary plow
On their steam locomotive
Had gone gunnysack
In that ethereal world

Where blizzards
Were invented
And crushing snow
Rushes in on you
Like vengeful banshees
Leaving you no choice

But to hunker down
And shiver
And hope for help.
So he and the crew
Ate up
All their sandwiches

Drank up
All their thermos coffee
Smoked up
All their Bull Durham
And ran up overtime
That bosses nightmared over.

I'm told he'd cowboyed
In Raton years before
After he got fired
From a line
Down in Arkansas
For his bad behavior.

Poems Without Rhyme or Reason and a Couple of Yarns

When Grandma
Moved up from Albuquerque
To sling hash
For the cowboys
He had to whip
All the bastards

On the ranch
Just to catch her eye
(He liked to claim)
And when he caught it
She let him know
She wanted out of there.

So he rode his horse
Up to Denver
Where David Moffett
Had an upstart railroad
That needed hands
And he spoke

To a foreman
Who asked him
If he could highball
Seeing as how
He looked
More like a cowboy

Than a hoghead.
Grandpa told him, yes,
He had railroaded
Out of Little Rock
To which the foreman replied:
"Then why ain't you

Still down there?"
To which Grandpa answered:
"Well, sir,
I was fired for fighting."
"For fighting?"
"Yes, sir, for fighting."

"So did you win?"
"Yes, sir, that I did."
"Well, that's the kind
Of man
We can use
On this railroad!"

So Grandpa and Grandma
Settled in Denver,
He gave the railroad
Forty-five years
And his family got new chairs.
See how it works?

And out
In his backyard
This old railroad cowboy
Took to growing roses,
Roses that leaped up
At you

Like fresh trusting faces
On little girls
Like new ideas
In a stagnant town
Like that one impossibly
Lucky turn of the cards

Which just won't come
But somehow does.
There were times
When it seemed
To me
That all he wanted

To do was roses
Unless I started
Talking baseball
And nagged him
Into the garage
To get a ball and glove

Dan Crane

Then he would throw
Heat at me
Until I went
Straight back to talking roses again,
Believe it!

When Grandma left
He bore up to it
Better than Judy.
In the end
He carried
The old dog

Out to his roses
Grabbed a spade
And planted her deep.
In the year
Or so he lasted
After that

He mostly fussed
Around in that garden
Of his
Sleeping upright in chairs
In his coveralls
Only a little bit drunk.

I go to Denver
Once or twice
A decade anymore
And when I do
I drive down the alley
Behind the old house

Full of new people now
With forty years
Of their own stories.
I don't know these people,
I don't want
To know them.

When I can see
They're not around
I like to stop
The rental car in their alley,
Step out to gaze
At the Rockies…

Then I walk slowly
To the high board fence
And peek over
At my Grandpa's roses,
Where for just a second,
The love reaches back.

Dan Crane

ONE LAST TRIP

Snowflakes and steam
Converge on pilothouse windows
Forming tears of resignation.

In the yellow light
Of a harbor in Sitka
I watch a man across the float
Dying in my sight
One blurry droplet
At a time.

He keeps a pillow
On his galley table,
The one soft thing
On that steel fortress.

He is up and down all night
As the pain of his cancer
Ebbs and flows
Out of synch with the tides
He has dealt with
All his fishing life.

So once again
A tough old sailor
Is out on the edge
His bow to the weather.

This trip will end soon
And money will go around
Faster than a gurdy.
People will school up
And make gull-shrieks

Like this old teapot
On my oil stove.

Meanwhile,
He just moves stiffly
About his chilly vessel
A befuddled commander
Tied fast to the dock
And going it alone.

Dan Crane

LOOKING BACK

I go
Where dead men
Used to fish.
I still recall
The graceful way
Their old wood boats
Would slice the waves.

They were better
At fishing
Than I am,
So I go
To their places
Hoping to catch
A feel

For how it was
With them,
How it was
To stuff the bellies
Of those pretty ships
With silver ingots
All stacked in rows.

Ballasted to the guards
They slide silently
Into the fogbanks of my memory…
You reach a point
Where you feel
More at home with dead men
Than live ones.

HOW YOU GET TO ALASKA

In the trunk of your car
You pack fishing gear
A box of hand tools
One rifle, one shotgun
Some camping gear
A few books and photos,
Changes of clothes
To meet the storms.

What you don't pack
Are broken promises
Cringing children
Bitterness and drunken envy
Gentle women with bruised faces.
They have already been shipped
Ahead of you
Wherever you are going.

You find yourself speeding West
On a gun-barrel highway
Across the grey sage-plains
Of Wyoming,
Parallel painted lines
In your rear-view mirror
Racing to converge
At a vanishing point behind you.

It is like viewing your life
In binoculars turned backwards,
The tendons of your memory
Stretching toward a blurry past

Then cramping before they snap
And forcing you
To relax the throttle
And take a breather.

You get a room
At the Moonglow Motel
Put the tab on plastic.
The place smells
Of perfumed cigars
And stomach throwbacks:
A shot of whiskey,
A dash of semen.

The T.V. flickers
With jumpy images
Of a preacher in polyester
Waving a born-again Visa card,
The bookmark in his Bible.
Another channel calls up
A shaggy satyr
Molesting a guitar.

So you open a window
With peeling paint
And admire
A ragged quarter moon
Tossed from the saw teeth
Of the mountains
Like a chip of ice…
And you fill your lungs with cold.

The castaway orbits
By inches
Held fast to the peaks

Poems Without Rhyme or Reason and a Couple of Yarns

By a pillar of light
Yet pushed away all the same,
The way porch posts
Stand between a first
And second floor.

And somewhere in the foothills
Haunting the half-light
A brash rebel colt
Banished from his herd
Circles on the edge…
Pushed outward by pride,
Drawn back by the gravity
Of stubborn loneliness

In the rough lumpy bed
You turn your mind loose
From its tether
And let it run
With the wounded moon
And the horses,
Past and present
Coupling on a bedsheet.

As for what's ahead
Yogi said it best:
"The future ain't what
It used to be."
You sleep on that thought
And let celestial strength
Pull blood through your tubes
And drag oceans

Dan Crane

Through all the channels
Of the world,
Flushing, flushing, flushing.
In the morning
You are fresh and strong.
The car starts quickly
And you follow the compass
On the dashboard pointing North.

Some days later,
Numb-assed and bug-bitten,
You top a hill
Near the end of the road,
A full moon washing
Ancient glaciers ahead,
A gleaming sea spread out
Beyond the borders of your mind,

And you are home.

WILD COUNTRY

I know places
Where you
Should not let me
Take you
Unless you chain
Your soul

To something heavy.
You will gaze
Slack-jawed
At water bursting
From limestone cliffs
Diving headlong

Into bottomless fjords,
Splintering into rainbows
As it plunges
And throwing light
On promises
You made yourself

In darkness years ago
But soon forgot.
If you go
With me
You risk losing
Your house

To a banker
Your lover
To a neighbor
Your job

Dan Crane

To a sycophant.
Maybe you should

Just stay home,
A warm drink
Beside your favorite chair,
A friendly and familiar
Stack of bills
Nearby.

GETTING AND SPENDING

Numbers take over my desk
Like a fat man
Who does intend
To be removed:
Make the money,
Pay the tax.

I divert myself
With poems
When figures get heavy,
Preferring similes to sums,
Images to interest,
Alliteration to calculation.

The poems and the ledgers
Side by side before me,
Left brain and right,
Suggest to me
A strange equation.

I wonder
If that insurance man
Who used to write
Was onto something
When he remarked
That money
Is a kind of poetry.

Dan Crane

FOR BIG DAVE
(who died asleep in Fairbanks)

You were too big
To be a stowaway
But Ron Rau
Shoehorned you aboard
At the last minute
Some years back

And we left Sitka
Looking for deer
Sleepy December deer
Easy pickings on beaches,
Their last refuge
From killing snows.

We named ourselves
The U.A.F. Hunting Team.
Four of us packed degrees
From there.
You packed a retirement stipend
And a used thutty-ought-six
With iron sights…
No more students
Or staff meetings
On your horizon
No more oxymorons,
No morons at all
Except us.

On my trips from helm
To coffee pot
You had a way

Poems Without Rhyme or Reason and a Couple of Yarns

Of jamming traffic.
Big guys on boats
Can do that
Especially when they bring
Goose-down clothes
And cameras and books
Full of pointy-headed stories
And poems.

Everybody got deer
Or saw some
Except you. I think
You might have been
A bit too noisy
Or maybe you got roped
By metaphor and hog-tied
By simile.

I wasn't with you
So I'm guessing.
I just know
That I wanted
To get you a shot
On the last day
Of that trip.

So I told you
To get into my skiff
For a trip ashore
And you upended
The damn thing
So it spilled you
And your thutty-ought-six
And left you looking

Dan Crane

Up at me from freezing water,
Your eyes as big as buoys.

Pulling on your arm
From the deck of that boat
With all your water weight
Was like trying to land
The primogeniture of halibut,
His tail made fast
To the anchor of a battleship
In sixty fathoms.

I cleated your arms
To my bulwarks
And piped the hydraulics
To a boom winch
Then at last up you came
By inches
Dazed and dripping.

I confess that I left you
Hanging a little longer
Than was called for,
Your feet barely touching
The deck
Your arms stretching skyward.

In the little time
We sailed together
That was the only control
I ever had over you:
Hanging you there
In my rigging
Like a trophy buck.

Poems Without Rhyme or Reason and a Couple of Yarns

Back in Sitka
You had stories to tell
And I had bedding to wash.
I remember
That we sang carols
By the Fishermen's Memorial,
Working in the names
Of everyone we knew
Who had lost his life
At sea,
Even recruited some drunks
From the Pioneer Bar
To help us in our cause.

I know you weren't anyone's
Idea of a fisherman, Dave,
But I still wonder
As you sang along with us
How close you had come
After your heavy plunge
To being sung about
Yourself.

You should probably know
The name of that place
I winched you out of:
They call it Deadman's Reach.
I'm happy to say
That I wangled for you
Another year or two of life,
But I truly wish

Dan Crane

That I had gotten you
A deer.

Poems Without Rhyme or Reason and a Couple of Yarns

BROKE-DICK RIDGE

"If you want me, look for me under your boot soles...I stop somewhere, waiting for you."
—Walt Whitman

My woman and I
Came to this place
When the snow
Was five feet deep
So we dragged our chainsaw
On a sled
And sweated in our snowshoes.

It took us an hour
To get to our summit
And we sucked air
A little less
Each time we did it.

Our trees were so dead
From beetle bores
That they almost snapped
When you started
The saw.

We banged them down
One by one and learned
That you can burn slash
On top of snow
Then come back the next day
And coax a fire back to life
In just minutes.

Dan Crane

We broke a lot of tools:
A peavey, a saw, an axe-handle.
Bigger things would follow
Like trucks and dozers and windows.
But the worst
Was the fire in our loins
That just smoldered along
Until it gave our place
Its name.

With spring
Our stumps stood four feet high,
Mockingly,
With two proud rounds
Of firewood each.
So we dobbed them down
And planted new life
Between them,
Birch and maple and pine
And flowers with crazy names.

It all came up
Well enough for where
It was, but really
Never overwhelmed us
With its zeal.

After several years
Our children came up
From the places
They had needed to go
And were kids no more.
But had mates now
With a hunger for place.

Poems Without Rhyme or Reason and a Couple of Yarns

So they looked past
Our scratching and clawing
With its struggling flowers
To a universe of ocean below
And topless mountains above,
Saw their own futures
On this stump ranch
And staked their claim.

Soon enough
They can plant us
With our crocus bulbs
And rye grass and clover,
Mix our ashes with volcanoes'.
We can only hope
That they remember to fertilize;
Moose nuggets work as well
As most anything…
And up here, like us,
They are free.

Dan Crane

FOR REBECCA YATES

The quiet words
You put into your poems
Still echo in our heads
As deeply as the ringing
Of a blacksmith's hammer.

You told us
About your winter
On a tired boat
In the Juneau harbor,
About the razor winds
From the Taku
Slicing through the seams
Of your lonely dwelling,
About the hard glaze
Stiffening your mooring lines
And making sheet ice
Of that little patch
Of sea you occupied,
About the lover
Who disappeared with the wind
When spring finally came.

You spoke to us
About your climb
To an alpine meadow,
How you put your hand
Under a rivulet
And walked away
Feeling as if you

Had touched
The tongue of God.

I quit doing poems
When you were at work,
Took up prose;
You don't send in a boy
To do a woman's job.
I read a story one night
To our tiny group of seekers,
Mostly old people
Looking for well-turned phrases
To ponder as they
Slowly exit this flesh.
You said you liked my work,
That I should try to publish.

I'm back at poetry again
Since you left us
And took your images
With you, images that flowed
So easily from you
Like music from Mozart
Or from that rivulet
On your mountain.

But I want you back,
We all want you back.
The stream you tapped
Is too far up the hill
For most of us to reach,
Being as far out of shape
As we are.

Dan Crane

All of us
Will try poems again
(Since you have gone)
In hopes of getting
Just a phrase or two right.
Give enough monkeys
Enough keyboards
And enough time…

Poems Without Rhyme or Reason and a Couple of Yarns

PUSHBUTTON CONTROL

As we motor to town
Paul Harvey tells us
That a man
Who takes exceptional pride
In his lawn
Has just gunned down
A neighborhood kid
For walking on it.

Our three dogs in back
Start barking as we pass
Others' pets near the road.
The noise increases
With each sighting,
To a point where
A jackhammer would sound
Like an oboe sonata
In comparison.

I add to the chorus of cacophony
With useless screams:
"Shut up, you idiots,
Or I'll put shock collars
On all of you!"

My wife says
That I would
Put shock collars
On everything in the world
If I could…

Now, there's a thought.

II.
SUSPEND YOUR DISBELIEF

Poems Without Rhyme or Reason and a Couple of Yarns

HARDSCRABBLE LIVES

Bear watching at the Yakutat dump is not for wimps. A blue-collar, dump-your-own affair on the ragged edge of the wilderness, it will never be discussed in slick brochures of the sort you see touting McNeil River or Silver Salmon Creek. You won't find a varnished log lodge or a cute little viewing gazebo anywhere near this spot. No one sets up T.V. cameras to pipe pristinely natural images across the miles to monitors in warm, carpeted museums. You just drive out to the edge of town, with or without garbage, when you get tired of drinking beer or laboring at hopeless tasks, and there they are...six or ten or fifteen brownies...slogging through rain and mud, snatching whatever they can from soggy fires fed by diesel fuel and plastic diapers, gouging their tongues on castaway soup cans, singeing their hair now and then, always bickering. Something like a scene from Dante's Inferno.

When I lived there twenty-five years ago, the dump was open 'round the clock. There were rumors about an especially nasty bruin that had met several people right at their trucks and hurried them along. Undaunted by such talk, though, I boldly took my own turn late one night when our trash can filled up, even brought my wife along as a witness to my unflappability. Slowly, with studied nonchalance, I upended the trash into a black pit imperfectly illuminated in the taillights. I could tell my witness was much impressed with my panache and my John Wayne swagger. I think she was totally won over when I casually flipped the can into the back of the truck, opened the door quietly, cracked a can of beer, and drove home without a word. No doubt I would have pulled it all off if I hadn't allowed her to carry the trashcan back to our porch when we got home. Sadly for me, it was still half full when she hefted it, and she nearly choked on her stifled laughter.

In the years that followed, civilization came along and dump hours were established: 7 A.M. to 7 P.M. Some said that this restriction sprang from the city's fear of tort liability. I have also heard it said that the new hours were a veiled attempt at population control and moral direction. You see, in a town without ball fields or movie houses or bowling alleys a good many of the townspeople can probably trace their own conception to stormy Saturday nights in that awful spot, not to mention that of their very own progeny. Such a dangerous, seductive ambience will always fall under government scrutiny, hence the new hours. Even so, bears remain free of the strictures that the rest of us must live by.

A case in point was the day last year when my deck hand and I drove out there with our boat garbage and found a dazed crowd of locals starting slack-jawed at an old boar that just five minutes before had smitten a smart-aleck cub with two or three vicious blows and killed him outright. Just that fast. The source of their argument had been a few fish heads lying in the ashes and muck, clearly unappetizing to me and certainly nothing to get killed over. We watched from thirty feet as the elder bear eschewed the fish but chewed the hapless cub instead, one slow mouthful at a time. If he was angry, you couldn't see it. He just lay there working on his breakfast: a cousin? a younger brother? perhaps his own son? As peaceful as a housedog with a soup bone. The crowd passed the story around for an hour or so as new patrons showed up, but the poor cub was nearly recycled and the story lost its drama, so everybody left.

A month later my wife and I took a couple of boxes of moose scraps from a recent hunt. We tossed the whole works a few feet in front of the truck in order to watch the picnic up close. Before long an old sow strolled over with her one remaining cub, and the show began. Not long after, my old friend John Pavlik drove up in a rusted truck with a twentysomething son and two-year-old granddaughter. Both men jumped out of the truck at once, left the doors open, and began pawing through garbage bags that hadn't yet been burned or shredded. For a while the men and the bears co-existed quite well since they were interested in different things, but when two huge boars emerged from behind a curtain of smoke, you could just feel the chemistry start to change. My wife got out of our rig and climbed into John's to sit with the little girl. Something was about to happen; she closed both doors.

"Goddamn bear heaven," John said.

"Maybe I should quit looking," his son replied.

"It's okay. I'll hold them off for a couple of minutes."

I thought John was about to pull a pistol from under his coat or, better yet, come back to his truck for a rifle. Instead, he just picked up a couple of big rocks, like baseballs, and climbed onto a little pile of rubble. As the sow moved closer, about fifteen feet, he went to banging the rocks together until she backed away. Within seconds, though, as if she were thinking, "Hey who's the bear here anyway?" she bolted back toward him, ears laid back and jaws snapping together in tune with the rocks. He immediately pitched one at her and connected obliquely, which was about as much as I could stand, so I jammed the truck in gear, popped the clutch, and landed squarely between them—a sort of referee without a whistle.

Now in a bare-knuckle scrap between a bear and a Pavlik I would put my money on the bear so long as it weighed at least five hundred pounds, but I'd never offer any odds. Their whole clan is famous from Sitka to Kodiak for grit and stamina, but also, I'm afraid, for bad luck. Years ago, when I first came into the country, the five brothers—Mike, John, Rudy, Andy and Paul—were without question the best seal hunters on the coast. That was in the sixties when you could just hunt and not worry about having to fake Native handicrafts. They have Native roots, to be sure, but beadwork wouldn't fit them any better than leotards would fit a walrus. All five of them were born with powerful bodies, almost like bears themselves, enough to make a high school wrestling coach tear his hair on learning that none of them ever spent much time in the public school system. Mostly they lived out their youth on a remote island scrounging up what they needed to eat: hunting, trapping, gathering, chopping wood, building shelters, and above all, fishing for everything that swims or crawls. They ran free in open skiffs, most often hatless and gloveless in any weather, shirts unbuttoned halfway down. From time to time I would see them with a load of seals or halibut, nets or crab pots, moose meat or even hay bales. Indeed, they kept horses at their place. Rudy, I'm told, was so into them that he once entered a Pony Express Commemorative race across the lower 48. Want to guess who won? Of course, their time on the island ran out, as did their youth, and they eventually moved to town under increasing pressure from the mighty hand of the U.S. Forest Service. Nobody has clearly explained to me yet why we are all so much better off for having that little island now uninhabited, their unheated buildings in disrepair, but I'm sure that someone in an office in Washington D.C. must know.

Mike was the first of the brothers I met, and the oldest. He wandered in and out of Kodiak now and then to sell his hides and restock his larder. I remember that he always won the seal-skinning contest at the King Crab Festival. It was said of him that he once rowed a Boston Whaler from Shelikof Strait to Kodiak city when his kicker crapped out, something like rowing a cement slab a hundred miles. One night in the parking lot outside Tony's Bar he busted three heads that everybody said were in need of a good busting and disappeared at midnight in his skiff with the wind blowing a gale and the rain just about slicing people in half. He always spoke softly, from what I could tell, but carried a big knife.

Not knife enough, though, to cut himself free of bad luck. In the years after I left that area I heard that he shipped out on an old wooden seiner that was trying to be something it wasn't, maybe a crabber or a tender. The thing broke apart on the way to Seward, and the search that followed turned up nothing. When his four brothers in Yakutat heard that the search had been abandoned, they jumped in the best skiff they had, with two or three drums of gas, and headed five hundred miles West, across the gulf in the dead of winter. The four of them scoured beaches all the way to Kodiak for over a month, siwashing through the long stormy nights beside driftwood fires and eating mostly from the sea. Somewhere around the Barrens they found a plank and a life ring. That was all. When they finally came home to Yakutat…salt-scalded, wind-whipped and frostbitten…a fool on the dock asked them how the weather had been. "Would have been nice to have some rain gear," Rudy replied.

You can be sure that none of them will ever go gentle into that good night. Last year Andy was working construction through the winter because fishing had gone sour but he still needed to eat. As he labored on a scaffold, bad luck fell off the roof and landed squarely on him breaking his ribs, puncturing his lungs, and just generally running him through a meat grinder. Of course, the man who fell off the roof was just fine. That seems to be how things go in the Pavlik world. As you would expect, Andy dusted himself off and finished his workday. When the pain kept him awake in a chair that night, he decided to check in at the local clinic next morning only to learn, after politely waiting behind a long line of hypochondriacs with runny noses, that the X-ray machine wasn't working that day. He was sent home with pain pills and told to check back the next day. When morning came he was medivaced, half-dead, to Sitka and painfully nursed back to life over the better part of a month. Choose a big caliber if you're looking for a one-shot kill on any of these people.

Some years ago Paul, the youngest, was assigned the job of tendering salmon from the Manby shore. The other brothers would stockpile their fish from Grand Wash and Esker Creek, then Paul would swing by and pick them up in a shaky old landing craft they had acquired somewhere, for cheap. Back and forth Paul would travel the thirty miles to town with one good load after another. It was rough duty because that entire shore is shallow and exposed to wind, but still, the boat was way cheaper than hiring a plane. The Pavlik's know those bars as well as anyone, but a landing craft is very clumsy in comparison to the light and lively skiffs they grew up with, so Paul bulled his way in there one ugly fall day, head-strong and fearless, and a brownish line of breakers pounded the boat and him to pulp. How do you figure that into the price of a Coho?

Paul's death reduced the Pavlik children by half because there was a sister, Mary, whom I have neglected to talk about. The fact is that I really never knew her because she didn't run that much with the men. She and my wife Carolyn became friends, though, because they both got pregnant at about the same time (but not at the dump) and thus were scheduled for regular visits to the clinic. When Carolyn advanced to the point where she worried the women in charge, she was sent to Anchorage for the stretch run, nearly a full month ahead of her time as things turned out, a costly and tedious experience. Mary fooled them, though; she managed to deliver a perfectly healthy baby right there in the village and then bled to death herself on a jet that wasn't fast enough. It has just gone like that for these beautiful people since they rolled onto the road of life like rocks from a crusher.

So…there I was between a dump grizzly with an attitude and a mountain man with a rock, snug inside my son's little red truck but wondering if my situation was truly as bizarre as it felt, or was just a routine Monday morning in the village. To my great relief, the bear huffed a bit then turned away. John dropped his weapon, and his son walked out of the hellish smoke, beaten. It was over; but still I had to know—and I'm sure you must be wondering—what could they have been looking for? I asked John straight out.

"Oh, the kid was cleaning house last night," he answered, "because he's getting ready to go on a vacation. He came out here with a few bags of trash, but when he got home to finish packing he couldn't find his Permanent Fund check and figured that he must have thrown it out by mistake. By the time he got back the damned gate was locked for the night so we had to wait until this morning."

"I'm sure he can get one re-issued," I said.

"That's what we figured. Trouble is, he's leaving tomorrow and needs the money in a hurry."

I didn't have an answer for that. I supposed they would work out something. My wife got out of their truck and back into ours. The Pavlik's drove off, and we sat there for a while pondering about what we had just seen.

With elbowroom restored, the bears went dutifully back to their grisly routine. After several minutes I finally backed away and turned toward town. Carolyn pretty well summed it up for both of us at that point.

"Dan," she said, "that would have made the best ad I've ever seen for direct deposit."

I couldn't disagree.

Dan Crane

AND HAST THOU SLAIN THE JABBERWOCK?

If moose deigned to write anything at all about men, they would have to include some mention of that bizarre behavior which marks the species in October: swollen necks, hysterical bellowing, hallucinogenic rushes through the brush.

...hacking my wobbly way to a road, I have suddenly capsized in mid-swing like a top-heavy ship. I am facedown in frosted mud, my shin freshly gashed, my harnessed neck sprained, my feet bound together by an alder branch. One hundred fifty pounds of steaming front quarter rests squarely in the middle of my back. Sunlight from the blade of my axe splinters into a miniature rainbow as it passes through an ice crystal on my eyelid. I am not, in reality, dying, yet groveling here a mere fifty yards from my truck, I am powerless to forestall an instant replay of man against moose—a montage comprising a dozen autumns at once. I blink away the rainbow and let the images roll. The glint of the axe arcs me back to that little silver trailer parked thirty feet from our rented tarpaper shack in Fairbanks...

It was forty below all winter, or so it seemed, and I spent most of the daylight hours (three or four) splitting firewood. My neighbor too would sally forth with his axe, but being an oil user, he had quite a different use for the tool. Beneath a tarp on his trailer roof lay six or eight granite boulders of meat—unbutchered, unwrapped, unlabeled—each piece about the size of a Volkswagen. His meat would keep all winter in such a cache (few of us had freezers before the pipeline), but he would have to gorge himself like a decadent Roman unless he wanted to live below a rotting mountain of meat come spring. Each afternoon he climbed a ladder, muscled a chunk of meat around, and split off ten of fifteen pounds in a single swipe, taking great care not to puncture his thin metal roof. Stew meat, burger, tenderloin—they were all the same to him. Within an hour the aroma of game meat and garlic and mushroom would waft through his steamy windows, at about the time I was heading inside to boil my Safeway hotdogs on the wood stove.

"Say neighbor," I shouted one day in March, "I've been coveting your moose meat all winter."

"Want some?"

"Oh no," I lied. "But I could use a few hunting tips for next fall. My wife and I are newcomers around here, and we struck out pretty bad last season."

"Is that your hunting rig?" he smirked, gesturing at my dented Ford station wagon with the muffler hanging loose.

Poems Without Rhyme or Reason and a Couple of Yarns

"Yeah. We drove every highway around here and never even got close to a bull," I apologized.

"You gotta have a four wheeler," he insisted, pointing with pride at his big blue Dodge 4 X 4. "I got my bull thirty miles up 'wipe out trail' and winched him right up to the truck. Winched the meat up onto the roof too. Only way to go."

...the icy water has found its way into my long johns and beyond. I manage to draw the uncut leg up under my chest. I reach my hand out for the axe-handle. Here we go, Amos...

Eskimo Amos had been sent to Seward from up North somewhere. They put a lot of old guys like him in nursing homes these days: before, they used to set them adrift on icebergs. Since Amos wasn't much for tiddlywinks and pinochle and since he was in remarkably good shape for an octogenarian, the people who ran the nursing home could see nothing wrong with letting him off the premises during the day. Mornings, winter and summer alike, you would see him trotting bowlegged along the road to the boat harbor, complete with jogging suit and watch cap—petting dogs, waving at kids, smiling at passing cars—his fishing pole in his hand. Evenings, his gait back up the hill would still be brisk, despite his string of cod, flounder, eel, sometimes even a salmon or halibut. In a bar one night I met an attendant from the nursing home.

"Say, how's old Amos been doing?" I asked, having missed seeing him for some time.

"He's fading pretty fast, I think. Just sits on his bed and looks out the window."

"That's too bad. The old boy sure does love to fish."

"Loves to hunt, too."

"Yeah. Say, what did he ever do with all those fish I'd see him packing up the hill?"

"Oh, he'd fillet them out and give them to the cook to feed the old people at home. Everybody figured it was good therapy for him. Pride in feeding a family and all that. Even when he brought too much fish, we just slipped it over to the hospital or took it home ourselves."

"Too bad he got so sick that he had to quit fishing," I pondered.

"It was the other way around," the attendant corrected me.

"How so?"

"Well, we had to keep tighter reins on him after he poached the moose. That was when he started getting sick."

"'Poached the moose?'" I stammered. "You'd better fill me in on this one."

"You see, the old people thought fresh fish was quite a treat at first, and the institution appreciated the savings and the breadwinner image that Amos had given himself, so everything was okay; after a few months, though, the old people got tired of fish and took to bitching through every meal. We had to tell Amos that he could only bring fish three days a week. He made the adjustment pretty well, I'll have to say, thanks to the woodpile. On his non-fishing days, he worked outside with a Swede saw and axe, stacking cords of wood to use in the social hall fireplace at night."

"But what about the moose?" I prodded.

"Well, like I said, the old people were bitching about the fish. Macaroni wasn't doing much for their dispositions either. They wanted meat, dammit, but the state could only afford so much on their budget, right? So Amos, on one of his woodcutting days, went out, without saying a thing to anybody, and killed this big cow moose that had been hanging around in the woods on the back part of the property all winter. Talk about strong! That old geezer walked into the kitchen and laid a whole hindquarter on the cook's butcher-block, and then he went back out to his work without saying two words. Christ, we had every official in the state on our backs before the week was over. Fish and Game wanted to hang him for illegal possession and hunting out of the season without a license; the local cops wanted to bust him for discharging firearms within the city limits."

"Firearms?" I asked. "Where did he get the gun?"

"That's just it. He didn't use a gun. He made a snare out of some old rope he found in one of the tool sheds."

"A snare, huh? What then, did he wait for the cow to choke herself of something?"

"Hell no! He let the critter flounder in the snow for a couple of hours and then bludgeoned her with the axe he was supposed to be using on firewood."

"And the school lunch program got a boost?" I second-guessed.

"Yeah, and Amos was declared loony and was put on permanent restrictions."

...I have my sore leg under me now. Easing my head out of the mud and looking ahead, I mentally amputate a branch and sidestep a rock. Fifty yards to go: a cakewalk, Amos. As I get up, I wonder which will hurt more—the shin or the neck. The shin wins, and when I lift the bad leg to ease the throbbing, the good leg rebels against the extra load and buckles at the knee. Tumbling over backwards, I glimpse my once new blue Dodge 4 X 4 on the road. Should have never sold the winch to buy those new tires. I am kicking on my back now like a berserk tortoise and bellowing frustration to the breeze. I could slip out of the pack now if I wanted, saw this quarter in half or bone it, and almost hop to the truck on one foot. Why don't I? For that matter, why

don't I move to Palm Springs and spend my dotage paddling an air mattress around a swimming pool? Oh God, the air mattress sequence...

Esker Creek had been steadily rising, my wife and I noticed, and by the third day of the hunt we began to have trouble cutting back and forth across it as we worked upstream to check for moose sign. It was tough country to negotiate—a vast post-glacial plateau where browse had sprouted through fractured rock. We were there to hunt, but both of us knew that packing through that brush would cast us as credible characters in a dramatization of some Siberian death march. The only true walking was close to the creek, where the banks were smooth and sandy, and our hope was to make a kill nearby. Now with the creek rising, from both an incoming tide and the torrents, which always accompany moose season on the coast, we were losing our only chance to hunt with rational logistics.

Our boots took the expected plunge, but we slogged on for another quarter mile anyway, resigned to being soaked for the day and not yet minding the extra weight of a gallon of water in each boot. Later, we remarked that the sound of four soggy boots plodding through muck ought to be recorded, patented, and marketed as a portable electronic moose call; for suddenly, through a wall of willows on the high bank to our left, the head of a young bull appeared: hackles erect, ears laid back, nostrils dilating and trembling—a nervous and pubescent youth entering the smoky foyer of a topless bar for the first time. We were the dancers. I raised my rifle quickly, then squeezed, reddening for a moment the rolling mist with moose-lust. He fell forward, literally brainless now, before I felt the recoil.

"Now I've done it," I moaned.

"What's wrong?"

"Well, in case you haven't noticed, that water is two feet deep already, and the tide hasn't even peaked. Ever try quartering a hippo in the water? Dead or alive, the results are the same."

"Hey, if we can roll him over on his back, I'll bet you can get him opened up and gutted while I race back to camp"

"But pack boards won't do us any good unless we can figure out how to cut him up without drowning."

"That's not what I'm thinking. I'll bet we can float him right out of here if we stuff an air mattress in his body cavity, wire it shut, and then inflate the mattress. I remember reading that trick somewhere."

"Must have been in *Outdoor Wife*."

"No, I think it was *Wield and Scream*."

"I guess it's worth a try."

Her scheme worked pretty well at first. After the tide change, though, the current became too swift for lining the animal from the banks, and so we tied him off to a tree and returned to camp for lunch. I pondered the situation for a while and came up with a new plan.

"You're going to ride on the moose?" she wondered.

"I don't see why not. It seems to have plenty of flotation and can only drift in one direction. I'll take an oar to fend off with."

"You'll get soaked to the bone."

"Already am. Keep a change of clothes handy. Let's load up the skiff; you can wait outside the surf line for me. I'll ride the whole thing right on out to you."

"Hawaii Five-O."

"Yeah, right here in Yakutat Bay. I'll pitch you a line once I'm in the breakers."

"Any last will and testament?"

"Naw, we'll make it."

We broke camp. I shoved the skiff away. The outboard started on the third pull, and she let it warm up for a full minute before easing it into "forward."

"Keep the bow into the seas and don't be shy about throttling though them," I called. "What ever you do, keep the boat from getting broadside."

But she knew that. She was running boats in Kodiak as a kid when the biggest piece of water in my experience was still a bathtub full of rubber duckies. The boat cracked the surf three or four times, shooting spray a good ten feet into the air each time, then she was through, bobbing softly on the long glassy swells. She cut the motor and waved me off. She would wait.

When I had untied the moose and got it drifting, I couldn't resist: I leaned back like a bareback bronc rider and pretended to spur with my hip boots. But the current soon speeded up so I quit clowning and gave all my attention to looking for the deepest water. No white water kayak, to be sure, yet this bloated, outsized raft of mine was maneuverable enough for these waters and not at all unstable, lying belly-up. It took less than an hour to drift the two miles to the bay. I figured the surf line at about fifty yards wide; the rope I had around the moose's neck, about ten. This meant Carolyn would have to come back into the mini-maelstrom to tow me on through. In fact, the breakers were only four or five feet high, not enough to excite an L.A. beach boy in the least, but dangerous nonetheless. An eighteen-foot skiff, poorly handled, could flip easily, I knew, but insofar as the moose surfboard was concerned, who could know? One thing I didn't like—and this was no joking matter—I was getting cold, water cold. There

Poems Without Rhyme or Reason and a Couple of Yarns

is no frostbite involved, just an easy numbing which ominously leaves altogether when your body heat drops to the point that your head goes stupid.

The first breaker turned me around—set me up, you might say—so that the second could pound me from behind. I had the line coiled and ready to throw but because my hand was numb I had to check my readiness for the throw by looking. The outboard was humming behind me now, getting closer, so I managed to turn around, telling myself again and again not to drop the coil. Carolyn charged toward me on the back of the third breaker. After it washed my glasses overboard, I blinked the salt from my eyes and studied our situation in that detached state of mind which follows panic—when you know you have only one chance to make the right move. I had known the same feeling twice before in near-misses on highways: a head on collision with a truck averted at the last possible second; snapping awake at the wheel in the middle of the night, soaring to lucidity at once on a rush of adrenaline, and dodging a guard rail by inches. "Don't swamp that motor," I heard myself shout, but she had already come off the back of the wave and powered around to meet the next one. We were unsynchronized for a few moments—she rising while I dipped again—so I withheld my throw. I looked her in the eye from forty feet when we suddenly caught the same rhythm. Her look said "now," and I pitched her a perfect strike. She made the line fast to her stern cleat, throttled up to take the slack, and we moved ahead as one. I wrapped both arms around the moose's foreleg, clenched my teeth against several more drenchings, and finally allowed myself to quit thinking as we drove at last through the surf and into deep water.

In the skiff I was peeled down to nothing, wrapped in blankets and sleeping bags, and granted invalid status. Carolyn ran the outboard for three or four hours while I slept and shivered. Finally we towed our winter's meat into the boat harbor and made it fast to the dock just like a boat. We could transfer it to the truck tomorrow. "All in all," she remarked, as I stumbled along the dock beside her, "that was the easiest pack we've ever had." And indeed it was.

...I'm on my feet again, accelerating. A fake to the left at the thirty. Stiff-arm an alder at the twenty. Ten. Five. Touchdown!

I flop the pack board on the tailgate, whispering thanks to the wheelgods in Detroit.

Maybe the craziest rolling stock of all was the bicycle-built-for-two. Fish and Game had long since outlawed the use of motorized vehicles on the old logging roads around Thomas Bay—fair chase and all that—so most of the Petersburg boys had pawned their Jeeps and ATV's at huge losses in favor of bicycles. Not the old Schwinns with fat tires either, but sneaky little French racing machines with gears enough to spirit vacationing schoolmarms from Tierra del Fuego to Dawson in one summer—in comfort.

Of course these bikes cost just a little less than I once paid my neighbor for a certain Dodge 4 X 4, and I naturally began to look for a cheap substitute. My kids gamely offered a wagon, a tricycle, and a learner's bike with training wheels, but I remained inconsolable. Then my wife—yes, the same one who had once invented a moose balloon—innocently suggested that I take her tandem bike.

"You mean you're going too?"

"You know I can't get away."

"But the thing is built for two people. I know I've seen you ride it alone, but shouldn't someone else be along?"

"It helps on the hills."

"Any ideas?"

"You might see if you can recruit Greg."

"I don't know. Look at the damn thing!"

"What's wrong with it?" she bristled.

"Well, for one thing, it's got no crossbars. It's a girls' bike."

"Sexist!"

"And what's more, it doesn't have any gears. And I see three or four things that ought to be fixed. My God, I can't do it! Look at that kiddy's seat on the back fender. Jesus!"

Greg and I managed, by cover of night, to sneak the contraption past the ruffians in the boat harbor. Quickly and silently we loaded it aboard my fishing boat *Eddie B* and buried it under tarps. We made the three-hour run across Frederick Sound the next morning, one day before the season opened. About a hundred feet from the end of the first logging road, we found a three-fathom trench and dropped anchor. There were already several other boats in the area. Our intention was to bicycle as many roads as possible that afternoon and decide where we wanted to be come morning. According to our maps, the roads criss-crossed a broad valley formed by a receding glacier. Other glaciers still clung fast to the mountains all around us. Moose or no moose, it promised to be beautiful country. The valley looked to be about three miles wide by eight miles long. The Patterson and Muddy Rivers were the main drainages, but numerous smaller creeks were shown on the map—all of them apparently unnavigable.

As we ferried the tandem bike by skiff from the *Eddie B* to a landing at the end of the road, we noticed a derelict Chevy pickup parked to one side. Someone had once erected on its bed a fifteen-foot plywood tower to spot from. The things people did before fair chase! We knew at once, on looking at the relic, that the alders grew thick in the valley.

"Maybe we should find a few boards, somehow fasten them to the fender, and raise the kiddy's seat," I quipped.

"Up yours."

We rode the bike around for a few hours, dismounting to check a few clearings for sign, picking berries, and talking to a few other hopefuls from town. Everyone agreed that they had not seen so many bikes (or so few moose) since leaving junior high. The laughing stock, of course, was our tandem rig. Loose gravel in the roads made for some heavy pedaling, and we suffered the indignity of being passed by anyone who wanted to pass. Most were polite, but others flipped us off as they streaked by, saying cute little things like, "beep, beep double trouble," or "I'll be hanged if I'll be banged."

"Call this hunting?" my partner growled.

"Uh, I think this is called scouting."

"Well, if you think you can get back to the landing alone, I'd like to follow this little creek across to the Patterson." He was pointing at the map. "It looks like there could be a clearing in here. I'll walk it out and then just follow the river down to that beach by where we're anchored. You can pick me up with the skiff in about an hour and a half."

I rode back to the landing alone, set the moosecycle's kickstand, and pushed the skiff off the beach. Glancing back at the derelict Chevy on its four rotten tires, I swore that a rust smear above one of the headlights looked exactly like a raised eyebrow.

"You said an hour and a half," I grumbled to Greg's flashlight, still unable to make him out.

"It's been closer to three."

"Yeah, I know. I got hung up watching a bull."

"Bull."

"I'm telling you, he's in there. Saw him bed down before I came out."

"Big?"

"Naw. 'Bout a three-year-old."

"Let's get back to the boat and have a snort."

Over supper, we laid our plans. Greg would leave me at the landing, then take the skiff back to where I had picked him up, walking in from there. Meanwhile, I would pedal up the road to where he had mutinied, and we would push toward each other, hopefully keeping the bull between us until one of us got a shot. We turned in at ten o'clock; by three the boat was surging hard against the anchor and a gail was screeching through the stovepipe like hell's breath. I got up and started the coffee.

"Christ," he groaned, "what bitch they going to name this hurricane after?"

"They've started naming them after men now. Besides, in Alaska it's just called wind anyhow. They'd run out of names in a year otherwise."

"Anchor holding?"

"So far. Think I'll let out a little more scope before we leave."

"Good. I'll find a tree to tie the skiff to."

"Coffee royale?"

"Damn right."

The bike had blown over during the night. Against the wind I found that I could ride only on the few flat stretches. Most of the way was uphill, though, and so I had to push the machine along as the rest of the pack streaked by me, not joking this time but dead earnest about getting up the road before daybreak. It was taking even longer than I had expected. When the first shots from up the road came blowing by me, I was sure I had to let Greg push the bull out to someone else. I finally got to our creek, where I found several other bikes jumbled together, and I lunged into the brush in despair. Less than three hundred yards from the road, I came upon six or eight hunters, among them Greg, gathered around a moose. I figured Greg for the killer right away because he was the only one doing any work.

"Damn," I apologized, "I couldn't get here any sooner. That worthless bike felt like it had square tires."

"It's okay. These guys spooked him back to me. Did you hear the shots?"

"Yeah, I counted three."

"The first was a desperation shot I made when I kicked him out of bed. Missed him by a mile. Then he ran this way until he had to face down the steel curtain you see here present. They had all bailed off at my first shot, I guess. Scared him right back to me. Bang, down he went. The third shot was just a *coup de grace*."

"I'll go back to the boat and fetch the packs."

"I'll stand guard. I hear the vultures come out of nowhere in this country."

"Got enough ammo?"

The crowd dispersed under our insults and by late afternoon we had moved all the meat to the road and were ready to roll.

"I don't know how much weight this thing can handle," I said. "Should probably haul just one chunk at a time with one rider."

"Fine. I'll strap that front quarter to the second seat and across to the kiddy's seat. You see what you can do with it."

"You mean you want to sit here while I make six more round trips?"

"But you're a lot better on that thing than I am."

"I've made two trips already today."

"Damn it, it's *your* bike!"

"Damn it, it's *your* moose!"

"Okay, we'll alternate," he relented.

"You first."

When we had the meat securely lashed, I gave him a final shot of blackberry brandy. He looked at me coldly, and I was reminded of other great stuntmen.

"Ladies and gentlemen! The fearless Awful Knawful will now attempt the descent of this precipitous logging road in the wilds of Alaska on his specially-built-bicycle-for-two. At the bottom of this natural ramp, he will attempt what no other man has ever dared, namely, he will endeavor to leap the tower on a derelict Chevy pickup and to alight unscathed upon the main deck of the *Eddie B.* May I have a round of applause?"

"Jesus," Greg mumbled in disgust, "I'm getting out of here."

He seemed a little unsteady at first, but within a few feet he found his balance and started picking up speed. I sat down beside the meat to wait my turn.

...not so bad. I'll wash and wrap the shin. Just have to ignore the neck. Trail's roughed in now, so I can leave the axe behind. Five more trips...

Greg came slowly up the road, limping and cussing, his pants torn and greasy, his lip split open.

"You wiped out," I greeted him.

"Whose idea was it to bring that goddamn bike?"

"Greg, it's the way they do it here."

"Piss on it. From now on I'm only going after ducks."

"What went wrong?"

"Well, I was coasting along just fine—downhill, wind at my back, really motoring—when I came to this little flat stretch, so I started pedaling just to keep up my speed. Whap! I wound my pant leg up in the goddamn chain. That hasn't happened since sixth grade. I figured I could just coast on down to the landing and stop with the front brake."

"Yeah, I forgot to mention that missing chain guard," I said.

"You also forgot to mention that the front brake doesn't work!"

"That too."

"Want to guess what I hit?"

"Another moose."

"Guess again."

"Another bike?"

"No. I hit the derelict Chevy. It's a good thing too. Otherwise I might be out there right now in twenty feet of water."

"How bad you hurt?"

"I'm okay, but the bike is totaled."

"No point in taking it back to Carolyn at all?"

"Forget it."

We packed that evening and the next day in the time-honored way.

...four more trips...

ABOUT THE AUTHOR

I came to Alaska in 1961, fairly disgusted with my life in Colorado but full of hope for our brave new world up here, a "young man green and lonely," in the words of John Haines.

After ten years or so as a student and a teacher, I underwent the biggest sea-change of all: I became a fisherman. Once you do that, it seems that you are never worth a damn for anything else.

Lately, though, a pencil seems less onerous than a gaff, so I am beginning to take the path of least resistance. This little patchwork book is the result of that weakness. I hope that you will try to like it.

978-0-595-39884-3
0-595-39884-7

Made in the USA
Lexington, KY
13 March 2010